CONTENTS

A JOURNEY IN REAL ESTATE – ARE YOU GAME?

PREAMBLE

Nobody would want to document how they decided to become a lawyer, doctor, engineer etc. In fact, if you are not a Gen Y or Z, you were probably given three choices by your parents in pursuing a higher degree and that is "you study to be an accountant, doctor, engineer" or such. Or some were given 3 choices of being "a doctor, doctor or doctor."

Many young people on the verge of going to college to pursue higher education would hardly think of real estate as a career or a choice. If they had, it would be scarpered by their parents.

Over the years, I am thankful and grateful that I have gone into this profession. It awarded such rich experiences for me in dealing with all kinds of personalities from my own negotiators to purchasers and owners. You wouldn't believe some of the characters I meet, some owners and some purchasers. Yet it brought in the "mullahs" to support my family and put three of my children through universities, one in Australia, one in Hawaii, and one in Atlanta. It also made me grow as a leader, brought out the confident and compassionate me. Made me understand what real estate is about and emphatised with my negotiators, their strength and conscientiousness etc.

After about 22 years in the profession, (at the point of writing), it set me thinking as to why young people or even laid off workers or even retirees do not consider this as a profession to go into. And ours, *according to the Board of Valuers, Appraisers & Estate Agents* is a profession governed under the **Board of Valuers, Appraisers, Estate Agents and Property Managers Act! WE** are supposed to be a profession like doctors, lawyers, engineers etc., as we have guidelines and rules for professional practices!

So, why aren't younger people and others not consider real estate as a career and profession?

Firstly, to obtain a license to practise, you need to sit for a Diploma in Estate Agency and then go for an interview with the Board. *Secondly*, upon obtaining the license to practise, you can open your own agency and have 50 negotiators straightaway working for you! Wow, you immediately become your own boss! And **thirdly,** *you need not report 9-5* and (most agencies are lenient) as long as you bring in the transactions.

The other thing that propelled me into real estate was that I LOVED LOOKING AT BEAUTIFUL houses! I would be showing clients homes and inside my mind I will be going like "Waah, look at that patio, the modern windows! I want!" or "Wow! Where did they get such artsy furniture!".

Like they said, if you have a passion for something (which for me, looking a beautiful homes), you will make a success of anything you do. Hmmmm.... Would looking at beautiful homes be considered a passion?
Surprisingly, the beginning journey was fruitful the first month! I close 4 deals! And that, with my heart in my mouth AND, my husband deciding to become a remisier at the same time! Two breadwinners of the family with uncertain incomes.

The reason I am writing this to give as comprehensive as possible what a career or choice in this profession totally involves.

WELCOME TO MY JOURNEY!!

GETTING OUT OF
THE 9-5 JOB

I was feeling more and more stuck in a 9-5 job and working in an IT company were long hours. I leave at 7 something in the morning and sometimes reach home at nine in the evening. I hardly get to see my children with my eldest son, 15 years old then, daughter 8 years and youngest, a son 6 years. I was feeling guilty and had this feeling that my daughter, 8 years old needed me to be there for her. She was already getting bullied in school and was vulnerable emotionally. I needed a job that could give me flexi time, send my kids to school and be more there for them.

I had an ex-colleague who left and joined real estate and I contacted her. She briefed me on what it involves and I made a decision to join her company. It was a hard decision as I was leaving a job with a fixed income to an uncertain income stream. My husband and I discussed this and I decided to go ahead. I handed in my resignation, went through the usual exit interview and I was OUT OF a 9-5 job!

Well, I felt a certain relief but also trepidation and uncertainty as what the future will hold for me. But I like the thought that I did not have to go to work at a fixed time.

I was eager to start and reported to work the next week.

Well, I was so used to a regimented time that I reported to work at

9am! Nobody was in except the admin girl and I waited for the license holder, who is also known as the principal of the real estate agency to brief me. The name of the company was Atlas Realty.

Those days, especially with small companies, they just throw you straight into the field and you have to land with both your feet on the ground. The principal just briefly explained that we rent and sell properties and to help me out, she gave me an account to do, that is looking for accommodation for Japanese clients. This was expatriate accommodation. She guided me into what locations were suitable to their requirements and budgets. I had to arrange a number of condominiums in good locations like Bangsar as their budget were between RM3,500 to RM4,500. This is 1994, and condos were considered luxurious pads with swimming pools and facilities. I had to fetch the Japanese expats from the hotels and drive them to the various units I have arranged in certain condominiums for their viewing. I remembered at that time, we showed Tivoli Villas, Cascadium, and Menara Bangsar. AND, for the first month of my career in real estate I closed 4 rental deals!!

It boosted my confidence and assuage worries about whether I will be able to put food on the table.

This direction, however, moved me into doing expatriate rentals. As I became more familiar with how to arrange accommodation to meet the expatriates' requirements, I was, most times able to arrange houses or condo units that they like. I dealt with Japanese, Americans, British, Australians and some days, I will be showing 12 – 15 houses/condos picking and dropping off 3 different groups. *I enjoyed it!* I made friends with some of them and we will have lunches or teas or meet-ups. They, in turn will introduce or recommend me to their friends or friends' friends who are transferred to Malaysia to work.

Of course, there will be some *dry* days where you are swapping flies and nobody calls. Initially, I worried and grind and worried. After a while, I realised that if I want to be in this business or profession long term, I have to learn to pace myself. If no one calls, or there are no deals that I am working on, I just go window shopping, maybe try and obtain more listings from owners or just chill.

I did well in expatriate rentals and income was good, some months nett to me RM20,000+

SIGNING UP FOR THE CERTIFICATE IN ESTATE AGENCY

One of the best thing I did when I came out, looking back, was that instincts told me to sign up to sit for the Board's exams to obtain a license to practise. I will detail the procedure later on how to sign up for the exams. I took night classes and at that time, it was known as the Certificate in Estate Agency and it took me 5 years to obtain the license. You can get a double degree in that time! This because you have to pass all 6 papers for Part 1 before you can move on to Part 2. I remembered I failed my Marketing (which I thought was easy peasy) and had to re-sit.

MOVING ON

After about 3 years with Atlas Realty and some internal problems, I decided to join another agency for further experience, doing sub-sales instead of just expatriate rentals. I was with Hartamas Real Estate for about 2 years plus and I passed my exams, went for my interview and obtain my license. At that moment, I don't know what I felt, relief? Or ecstatic? I couldn't tell. During my time in Hartamas Real Estate, I gained further experience in doing sub-sales and found that deals were not as forthcoming when I was doing expatriate rentals. I had to source for listings and be continuously looking out for properties for rent or sale.

OWN BOSS

I was ecstatic upon obtaining my license to practise! IN the year 2000, I opened my own firm, ***Asian Land Realty Sdn Bhd.*** Started off with about 4 – 5 negotiators and grew to about 15 negotiators within 2 – 3 years. Those were the times of good property market. Over the years, the market would be up and down but I ***always tell negotiators that if you set up your strong foundation within the 1st two years,*** *you will always be in business. AND I believe service is utmost important as clients will recommend clients.* The other thing is to acquire as many listings as possible.

Over the years, my agency grew with branches in Johor and Penang, but closed down due to management and dishonest negotiators. Now I only have a branch in Kucing. I have 3 license holders who joined Asianland and remained.

WHAT HAS EVOLVED IN THE REAL ESTATE INDUSTRY

As I am writing this, I have been doing real estate for 25 years and have set up my own agency for 19 years. A lot of things have changed and evolved over the last 25 years. What are there?

- When I first started real estate, there were no hand phones and computer was something rare. We advertised our properties for sale/rent in The Malay Mail (at that time) and later The Star. That was the way you could get clients and business. NOW, it is *social media.* Internet, Facebook (some call it Bookface), website, Instagram (*what is that???), Wechat, SMS blasts, Whatsapps etc...* Newspapers ads dropped from 14 – 15 pages of Classified Ads (property section) to 4 – 5 pages (Yes! I counted the pages)!!

- Where we used to approach developers to appoint us to market and sell their projects, NOW, it is how many units you can underwrite. AND they are talking about properties with returns potential, though many investors got stuck with their investments once the instalments kicked in and returns period ended. That is another story or stories.

- In Sept 2013, (and I am very happy with this), the Board of Valuers, Appraisers and Estate Agents came up with the ruling that all who want to do real estate as a career and join real estate agencies have to sit for a 2-day course known as the ***Board of Valuers, Appraisers, Estate Agents & Property Managers Negotiators Certification Course (BOVEAP NCC)*** and obtain a REN tag in order to be able to join a real estate agency to become a negotiator. Prior to this, the Board did not recognised negotiators and the license holder is liable and responsible for any wrong-doings by their negotiators.

- Doing real estate now is so different from 25 years ago. Social media has changed many things and there are now so many different schemes and connotations of investing and purchasing properties. Prices of properties have also appreciated, some areas, more than a 100%. E.g house I bought in 1999 at RM250,000 is now RM1,600,000. Obtaining bank loans are now a challenge.

- Facing challenges of getting negotiators on board as some real estate agencies who have funders or cash rich investors are offering as high as 98% commissions (?!) and underwriting bulk purchasers of properties for their negotiators to sell and bringing in foreign buyers.

CAN STILL DO AH?

I still enjoy real estate, and realised this when I had to handle a recent property for a client personally. *If you are thinking of being your own boss, now keen to be tied down to a 9 – 5 job, enjoy freedom of movement, want to have BIIIG income, then THIS IS FOR YOU.* Some say "can still do meh?". **CAN.**

It may be more challenging in the present times, but there are always cycles and I believe if you know how to manage it well, IT IS A GOOD CAREER! Even into your old age!!

HOW TO BECOME A CERTIFIED REN (REAL ESTATE NEGOTIATOR)

STEP 1

Attend a 2 days Negotiators' Certification course with the Board of Valuers, Appraiser, Estate Agents and Property Managers. Check their website who are the providers of such courses. The institute or provider will accord you a certificate at the end of 2 days. With this certificate you can join any estate agency.

STEP 2

Join any agency you choose, and the agency will obtain the REN
tag for you.

HOW TO BECOME A REGISTERED ESTATE AGENT

STEP 1

Enrol either with affiliated universities or institute who either have in-house diploma in estate agency course, or tuition courses conducted weekends or in the evenings. You have to pass Part 1 and Part 2, of which you are given 3 years each part to pass all six subjects. After passing both parts, you will be known as Probationary Estate Agent (PEA).

STEP 2

You now register with the Board as PEA and have to undergo a 2 years practical training with an estate agency registered with the Board. During these two years, you will have to do two work papers, one on a project and one on an individual sale. Daily log diary is also required which has to be signed and vet through by the principal of your agency. At the end of 2 years, you will then register for an interview with the Board. Once you pass the interview, you will obtain your license to practise and is a registered estate agent.

WELL, HAPPY JOURNEY FOR THOSE CONSIDERING!!

Copyright by : L C Seow

Seow Lee Chong, (L C Seow) , founder and Managing Principal obtained her certificate to practice in January 2000 and is registered with the Board of Valuers, Appraisers & Estate Agents. She started real estate in 1994.

Asian Land Realty was formed in January 2000 when L C obtained her license to practice after about 6 years of practical experience on the ground.

During these practical on the ground experiences, she handled expatriate accounts, sales and rentals of residential and commercial properties, industrial properties and has built up a solid clientele base, both buyers and sellers. In her 16 years of experience in real estate, L C has expanded to project marketing and sales, and foreign property investments. From a 6 negotiators force, Asian Land Realty has grown to a force of 60 negotiators.

L C has served in the Malaysian Institute of Estate Agents (MIEA), first as a councillor and then as Secretary General from 2002 to 2005. L C is also the Course Director of her training company for real estate, Starfish Training Sdn Bhd.

One of the projects

WELCOME TO REAL ESTATE!

www.ingramcontent.com/pod-product-compliance
Lightning Source LLC
Chambersburg PA
CBHW050803290526
45792CB00008B/2305